Enneagram

Find your Strengths, Improve Your Weaknesses, And Reveal Your True Personality

By Lara Chapman

Table of Content

Introduction

It is a hollow existence going through life without truly understanding the inner workings of your being. Without truly understanding the things that you like and do not like. Without understanding the motivators that drive you and give you a sense of purpose. Without knowing why you get out of bed every morning and why you should look forward to another day.

Unfortunately, this is the reality that most people face. They drift through life every single day, building a shell of a person and not knowing why they are on this Earth. That is no way to live. In fact, that is not living at all. It is simply an existence, like a pebble existing along the road side.

To live a life that is full of happiness, fulfillment, and to have a sense of achievement, you need to truly discover the person you are so that you can walk the path that you were meant to walk. A life lived without finding the courage to understand yourself will lead to regret and a lot of wasted time that could have better served. To ensure that this does not happen to you, you need to go on a journey of self-discovery.

Self-discovery is the process of becoming self-aware of your true potential, character, motives, and values. This journey involves proactive events in a person's life in an attempt to discover their priorities, how they feel about themselves and the world around them, and their spiritual beliefs. This person attempts to live life based on their own preferences rather than the opinions of others around them such as family and friends. Going on a journey of self-discovery is about finding yourself.

If you are unsure if you have started a journey of self-discovery, here are a few questions to ask yourself:

- Do you doubt yourself in the company of others or feel scared if someone opposes the same sort beliefs that you believe in?

- Do you find yourself frequently trying to convince others about your beliefs, thinking that the more people who believe it the more truthful it becomes?

- Do you frequently try to find groups of people that believe in the same things that you do so that you can have the security of that group?

- Do you fear leaving the groups that you associate your identity and beliefs with?

- Do you often resist change or discovering a new truth about yourself?

- Are you inflexible at incorporating new understandings and beliefs into your current beliefs?

- Do you often cling to the familiar rather than get out of your comfort zone?

- Do you often find yourself trying to convince yourself about certain things like the fact that you enjoy your job?

If you answered yes to more than 50% of these questions, this is a cause for worry. In fact, it indicates that you do not know yourself very well and that you do not have a firm foundation of who you are as an individual. Often times, it is hard to face the realities of who we are as individuals. You may discover some ugly truths about yourself. The great thing about discovering them is being able to change them. The only way to change these things is to have that self-awareness and acceptance and move in the direction to do something about it.

On the flip side of the coin, you may realize some wonderful things about yourself - the things that make you worthy of being a human being and the things that pull other people towards you.

Unfortunately, you will never know these positives and negatives if you do not take the time for introspection and self-discovery. The reality is that no one else can do it for you so you need to make that decision to take the journey that might be hard but also fruitful and rewarding.

Why Self-Discovery and Understanding Are Important

Self-discovery is not a coin with two sides. It is multifaceted and it is a journey that will take the rest of your life because life is a process of evolution and change and every human being on this earth changes daily. Every second, you are exposed to new things, new experiences, new ideas, new thoughts, and new feelings, and every one of these has an impact on you as a human being and on your character.

Self-discovery is about finding your purpose in life so that you do not wander aimlessly. It is about digging deep into your mind, heart, and soul to find the things, both good and bad, that shape you as a person. It is about realising your beliefs and standing firm in them no matter the obstacles or barriers that you may face. Ultimately, self-discovery is about finding happiness, fulfillment, clarity, and enlightenment in yourself.

As I mentioned before, this will not be an easy journey. It will involve confrontation of yourself and people in your life and maybe even the environment that you exist in. You will have many moments of fear, of doubt, of confusion, and of misunderstandings. You will have your emotions stirred repeatedly and some of the beliefs that you held onto previously will become unhinged. You may realize that some relationships that you have are toxic to your development as a human being and that you may need to cut or limit the ties that you have with certain people or groups. On the other hand, you may need to foster other relationships that make you a better person.

On this journey of self-discovery, you will become angry, sad, frightened, and a host of other emotions that most people do not like to deal with. However, you will also find that you will become a lot calmer, that you will find joy in even simple things, and you will stop having unrealistic expectations of other people and yourself. Therefore, you stop setting yourself up for disappointment because you have more insight into your individuality and are more perceptive of the character of other people.

To break it down into simpler terms, here are a few of the benefits you will gain from discovering who you truly are:

- It allows you to heal from past trauma and childhood issues. Many people develop unhealthy attachments and beliefs due to past trauma and childhood issues. These often have lasting impressions and make us form unhealthy patterns that inhibit our progression and development as human beings. By taking the time to discover yourself, you can move past these roadblocks to a new, improved, and better you.

- It keeps you from feeling alone. Human beings thrive on connectivity with others but when you connect with yourself on a deeper level, you become more comfortable with yourself and start to enjoy your own company. Therefore, you will never truly feel alone and can appreciate the connection you form with others even more.

- Self-discovery gives your life meaning and direction. A life filled with fulfillment and joy is one where an individual gains knowledge and insight from every experience and connection that this person has. It allows a person to grow mentally, spiritually, and emotionally. This person does not hope that the pieces with just fall into place but actively seek experiences and connections that benefit them and help them grow even more. By doing this, the person gains a sense of purpose.

- Being on a journey of self-discovery allows you to control your own destiny and to create your own reality. Most people are unhappy with their everyday lives because they allow someone else to control their destiny, such as their family, friends, and bosses. Discovering yourself and being aware of your wants, needs, and desires on the deepest level allows you to take the reins and empower yourself to shift your overall energy to one that manifests the things that you want rather than being accepting of the things that happen because others had control over it.

- Self-discovery encourages self-confidence. It brings out the uniqueness in you and allows you to see what makes you special and perfect in your imperfections. You begin to love yourself more and feel more secure in who you are as a person.

Oftentimes, we are our own worst enemy. We lie to ourselves about ourselves. We make false judgements on who we think we are, the things we feel, and the things we accept about ourselves and other people. Discovering yourself and understanding the inner workings of your mind, heart, and soul allows you the freedom to feel how you feel, to think how you think, and to simply be the person that you are and not a mold of what anybody else thinks you should be. That freedom is priceless and is something everyone should know before their life comes to an end.

How to Start a Journey of Self-Discovery

There are many ways a person can go on a journey of finding the inner workings of who they are as a person but one of the most effective ways is through the Enneagram. This type of journey to self-discovery has been around for centuries and its longevity stems from its effectiveness. This book is about helping you use this tool to understand yourself on a level that is complete and holistic.

I want to thank you for getting this book and for having the courage to face this journey that may at times be lonely. Take comfort in the fact that, in the end, you will become a better person for it and you will love and value yourself as you are.

Chapter 1: What is Enneagram?

The Enneagram is a system of nine personality types based on the combination of modern psychology and traditional methodologies. This tool is not only useful for understanding ourselves but for understanding the other people in our lives as well. It has three major applications and they are:

- Personal growth and spiritual development

- Leadership skills development including team building and communication skills in business applications

- Success in personal and professional relationships

This system allows you to work more effectively in these areas because it allows you to increase your self-awareness and therefore, your emotional intelligence as you engage yourself and your environment. You are no longer ruled by emotions or patterns of thinking that affect your mood and therefore, the way you behave. Increased emotional intelligence allows you to build successful relationships with friends and family, and in your professional environment. This intelligence also allows you to support your character strengths and identify the qualities which are weaker and need development.

Before we delve into the history of the Enneagram, let's dive deeper into what it truly is and why it has survived centuries and is still so effective.

What Is Enneagram?

Enneagream is also called the Enneagram of Personality. The word Enneagram is derived from the Greek words ἐννέα (ennéa), which means "nine" and γράμμα (grámma), which means something "written" or "drawn." The Enneagram is based on a model of the human psyche with a foundation of understanding the typology of nine interconnected personality types. These nine personality types are represented by the diagram below.

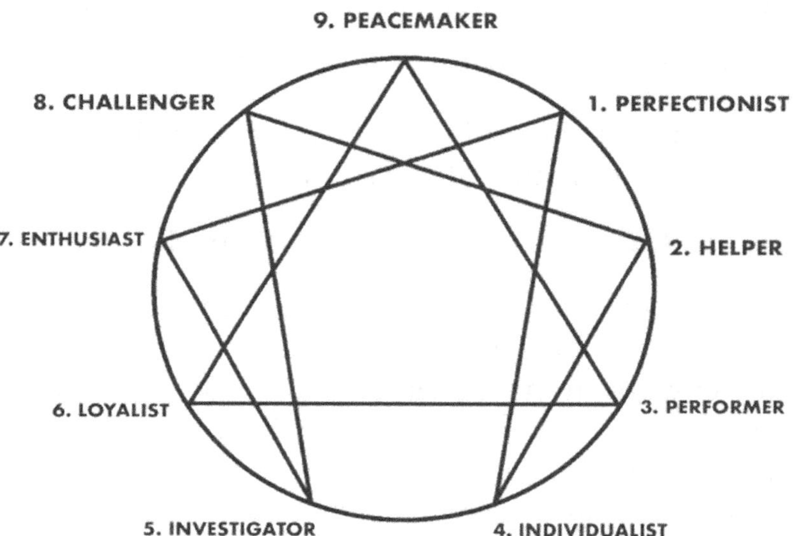

At first glance, the structure of the Enneagram can seem quite confusing and intimidating. However, on closer examination, it can be seen that the structure is simple. The nine points are of equal distance apart along the circumference of the circle and each is designated a number from 1 to 9 with 9 at the top. Each point represents one of the nine personality types and each is interrelated with the other in specific ways. This interaction is indicated by the inner lines of the structure.

The nine personality types in numeric order are:

1. The Reformer

2. The Helper

3. The Performer

4. The Artist

5. The Observer

6. The Loyalist

7. The Enthusiast

8. The Protector

9. The Peacemaker

What is a Personality Type?

A personality type is a psychological classification of different types of individuals so that personality traits can be distinguished. These traits usually occur together consistently, especially when they conform to a certain pattern of responses.

For example, introverts and extroverts are two fundamentally different categories of people due to the traits they exhibit. However, introverts and extroverts are part of a continuous dimension, with many people falling in the middle of the spectrum.

Personality traits fall into one of the following 5 categories:

- Openness. This is also called openness to experience and people who register high in this trait are highly adventurous, love new experiences, and are curious. People who are very open often live by the philosophy that "Variety is the spice of life." On the other hand, people who register low in openness are the opposite and prefer to stick to their habits and avoid new experiences.

- Conscientiousness. Conscientious people are very organized and have a great sense of duty. These people are very goal-oriented and disciplined. To sum it up, conscientious people are planners and very dependable. People who are low in conscientiousness are more spontaneous and carefree in the way that they live.

- Extraversion. This trait speaks to how outgoing a person is. People who register high in extraversion are called extroverts and are what you might call the social butterflies in group settings. They draw energy from being in a crowd and are very chatty and assertive in social interactions. People who register low in extraversion are called introverts and prefer to be alone most of the time because their brains find it very difficult to process social interactions. Their energy gets depleted by being in large groups. Introvertism is often confused with shyness. However, shyness is a fear of social interaction.

- Agreeableness. This is a measure of how approachable a person is. A person who is high in agreeableness is often kind, warm, compassionate, and helpful towards others. Other people find it easy to trust such a person. People who are disagreeable are not as easily approached because they are less likely to cooperate. Disagreeable people often find other people suspicious and are often cold in their demeanor.

- Neuroticism. Neurotic characters are people who often obsess over things and display high levels of anxiety. Neurotic people often suffer from depression. On the other hand, people who score low in neuroticism are more emotionally stable, worry less, and tend to be less anxious.

The History of Enneagram

The origin of the Enneagram is unclear, and there are many theories as to where its roots came from. Despite the disputes of the origin of the Enneagram, all the theories seem connected through spirituality and specific mathematical and philosophical traditions.

Here are the theories that try to explain the origin of the Enneagram:

- Some historians believe that the Enneagram was part of the Pythagorian culture and dates back to over 4,000 years. This theory is supported by variations of the Enneagram symbol which supported sacred geometry back then. This line of mathematical thinking was passed on through Pluto, his disciple Plotinus and other neo-Platonists. They speak of nine divine qualities that manifest themselves in human nature.

- Others believe that this system came into the esoteric Judaism through the Jewish neo-Platonist philosopher called Philo because it appears as the Tree of Life in the ancient text for the symbol of nine foldness. This ancient text is called the Kabbalah.

- There are other speculations that the symbol appeared in Islam Sufi traditions as it was referenced in the Naqshbandi Order, also known as the Brotherhood of the Bees.

- The possibility of the Enneagram having esoteric Christianity roots has been discussed because of medieval references to the Evagrius' catalogue of various forms of temptation called Logismoi. This was later translated into the seven deadly sins.

- Ramon Llull (1232-1315) was a mathematician, polymath, philosopher, logician, Franciscan tertiary, and writer from the Kingdom of Majorca. He tried to integrate the different faith traditions using a philosophy and theology of nine principles.

- In the 17th century, an Enneagram-like drawing was found in the literature created by the Jesuit mathematician Athanasius Kircher.

In more recent times, Russian teacher, George Gurdjieff (1879-1949) used the Enneagram system to explain the laws evolving around the creation of the universe. The roots of this theory are much clearer compared to the others and Gurdjieff called it a symbol of Perpetual Motion. Gurdjieff mentioned that he was introduced to the Enneagram in the 1920s after he visited a monastery in Afghanistan.

Bolivian-born founder of the Arica School, which was established in 1968 in South America, Oscar Ichazo, also taught the Enneagram. His theories and teachings on the Enneagram of Personality formed part of a larger body of work which he called Protoanalysis. He exposed this work to a Chilean psychiatrist named Claudio Naranjo and through their efforts the Enneagram became part of modern psychological traditions. Also, through the efforts of persons like Bob Ochs, who studied with Naranjo, the Enneagram was introduced to several Christian communities in the United States. The system gained much more exposure through the writings of authors like Don Riso, who was the head of the Enneagram research and study in New York City and who wrote the book, *"The Wisdom of the Enneagram: The Complete Guide to Psychological and Spiritual Growth for the Nine Personality Types,"* which is co-written by Russo Hudson. Other famous authors that wrote on the subject of the Enneagram are David Daniels, Jerry Wagner, Mark Bodnarczuk, Sandra Maitri, Beatrice Chestnut, and Ginger Lapid-Bogda.

Ever since it has been put into the spotlight like this, the Enneagram has been validated through experimental and empirical studies. It has also been cross-referenced with other constructs of psychology such as the MBTI, which stands for Myers-Briggs Type Indicator. The MBTI is a system of taking personality inventory through an introspective self-report questionnaire. The results of this questionnaire allows an individual to discover the differing psychological preferences in how he or she perceives the world around them and make decisions based on those observations. The MBTI was constructed by Katharine Cook Briggs (1875–1968) and her daughter Isabel Briggs Myers (1897–1980) and was based on the conceptual theories of the Swiss psychiatrist, Carl Jung (1875–1961).

Using the Enneagram for Self-Understanding and Discovery

As mentioned earlier, the Enneagram describes nine distinct personality types. Each personality type is characterized by distinct mental and emotional traits. These mental and emotional characteristics help define the way the owner of the personality type thinks and feels. This therefore, influences the life experiences that this personal will have.

Personality types are so important that they have defined the persona that we carry throughout our lives. This personality type defines the way that a person thinks and feels about him or herself, how he represents him or herself to the world, and how he or she perceives the world around them. In essence, your personality type is your true-self and is a description of the inner landscape that shapes you.

Personality type and personality are two terms that are not to be confused. While your personality type is a fixed condition, your personality, which is also called your ego, is conditional and changes with your environment. Since our environments are always changing, so do our personalities. Your personality type however remains grounded no matter what you go through, who you meet, or what day it is.

This is important because it shows that no matter how much your environment changes or how much you grow and evolve as a person, the center of who you are as a person remains the same. This knowledge allows you to gain confidence as you embark on a journey of self-awareness and self-discovery. You will know that who you are today will fundamentally not be different tomorrow or any other day no matter what life experiences you go through.

Also, knowing your personality type can help steer you in the right direction to discover your strengths and weaknesses, the things that make you feel happy and fulfilled, and knowing how you can strengthen your weaknesses.

Understanding your personality type is not so that you can be forced into a mold. Instead, it is a useful tool for better understanding yourself and how you relate to other people. With this understanding, you can approach the journey to self-discovery knowing that your traits that need to be reformed can be done and that you can strengthen those that make you a great individual for others to be around. This will ultimately make you a happier person who is mentally stable. With mental stability comes the increased likelihood of better physical health.

How the Enneagram Can Help You Develop Your Relationships

The Enneagram is not only founded on psychology but is a means to deeper spiritual understanding of one's self. This system can be a source of insight into your mind, heart, and soul so that you can gain the wisdom to make good life choices that can enrich you as an individual and enrich the relationships that you form with other people. Knowing your personality type can help you become a more effective communicator and communication is at the heart of every relationship that your form, whether it be personal or professional.

Communication involves the exchange of information between two or more persons. However, communication is not just about what is written or said. Often times, it is what we do not say that has the most impact on how effective communication is. Our body language and how our spirits interact has a big part to play in how we transmit and receive information from each other. The Enneagram allows you to gain greater insight into why and how you communicate with other people. This knowledge can allow you to develop strategic approaches to the way that you seek out and interact with other people so that you can act in a manner that is most effective when it comes to imparting to your feelings, ideas, and thoughts to others.

The Enneagram allows you to also understand how you influence others so that you can adjust your communication style to suit your audience and even increase your circle of influence. This can help you become a more effective leader because you understand the different needs of the people around you and you understand your strengths as well as theirs. This allows you to empower yourself and to nourish growth and performance. Part of being a good leader also involves strategic thinking and decision-making. By being aware of your personality type, you can be more aware of your core motivations and what drives you to increase the quality of your life and those around you.

All of this helps you develop a character of finesse. Since you have this insight into the character of others, you can better anticipate their reactions and approach communication in a way that keeps the interaction as friendly and as insightful as possible.

At the core of it all, building better communication skills helps you build stronger, long-lasting relationships with not only yourself but with your friends, family, colleagues, and others. This encourages skills of objectivity and compassion so that you can not only draw out your own strength but those of the people that surround you. Gaining insight into the Enneagram makes this process a lot easier and faster for you.

Chapter 2: The Enneagram Personality Type 1 - The Reformer

This personality type is also called the Perfectionist or the Improver. Type 1s are driven by the motive to be right or to be good. The need to improve themselves, others, or situations are always focused on correcting errors. In fact, this personality type is fixated on improvement. They are constantly looking for ways to make things better because to type 1s nothing is ever quite good enough as it, hence why they are often called perfectionists. Because of their responsible nature, Reformers often take on high responsibility service roles and occupations such as teachers, health workers, and ministers.

What Makes the Reformer a Great Personality

1. *The Reformer has a high ethical standard.* They make very responsible and capable friends, colleagues, and partners. They also tend to be very loyal people who are highly principled and competent. Their competency lies

in the fact that they love to follow rules and expect others around them to do so as well. Because they are so strong in their convictions, they are often excellent leaders who have the ability to inspire others to follow their own vision of excellence.

2. *The Reformer is highly self-disciplined.* Reformers are natural-born list makers and organizers. They are also very driven and ambitious, often falling into the category of workaholics. They are practical and proactive people that get things done, often the last one to leave the office and the first one in every morning.

3. *The Reformer has a fine eye for detail.* This person is great at bringing order to chaos because of their ability to see flaws in others, themselves, and situations. This can be beneficial for making improvements and finding solutions.

4. *The Reformer is responsible.* Because the Reformer is such a level-headed, mature person, they are great potential moderators between parties that do not have such a high level of consciousness. Because of their responsible nature, Reformers are also ones to delay gratification, waiting until all their responsibilities and to-dos have been completed and checked for before allowing themselves to partake in any activities strictly for the pleasure of it.

The Deadly Sins of the Reformer

1. *Reformers are rigid in their self-control.* Because of the Reformers' need for perfection, they often feel guilty for

falling short although the expectations for themselves and the expectations that others have of them may be unrealistic. This often leads to anger at themselves and the world around them. The Reformer often suppresses this anger because it is seen as a bad emotion and Reformers are wholeheartedly striving to be good. Due to this suppression, Reformers can have bursts of temper tantrums. More often though, this anger manifests itself into other emotions such as impatience, annoyance, frustration, and a judgmental attitude. This suppression of anger can be very damaging to the relationship the Reformer develops as their communication with others can come off as overly harsh and critical.

2. *Reformers are emotionally repressed.* Due to their never-ending pursuit of perfection, Reformers have a very hard time relaxing and often deny themselves the small pleasures of life. This can be emotionally taxing hence why Reformers often repress their emotions because they have a hard time expressing them. This discomfort comes from their idea that showing emotion is a sign of weakness and a lack of control. Type 1s are hardly ever spontaneous even though they have the tendency to have multiple interests and talents and hardly ever run out of things to do.

3. *Reformers demand impersonal perfection.* Reformers always demand perfection in both themselves and others. Due to this demand and their ability to repress their emotions, this makes Reformers people that are difficult to live with because of their very high standards and their cold approach towards other people when their need for perfection is not met.

4. *Reformers suffer from judgmentalism.* Because Reformers have such a fine eye for detail, wanting things to be "perfect," they over analyse others and themselves and this can become quite burdensome on the Reformer and those around them.

How Reformers Relate to Other Personality Types

Reformers vs. Type 2s

Reformers relate very well with type 2s, who are also called Helpers. In fact, they are a complementary pair. If a relationship of any capacity is formed between two such personality types, it is built on shared values. Helpers bring nurturing and caring qualities to a relationship while type 1s bring responsibility, consistency, and integrity. Despite the great complementary pairing, there is still the potential for confrontation between these two personality types because Reformers have a need to work first, play later and keep themselves and others very much in check. On the other hand, Helpers can see this as being too impersonal.

Reformers vs. Type 3s

Both of these personality types are competent, serious-minded, and task-oriented. As a team, they can accomplish many great things because of their high energy and need to succeed. Trouble arises in a relationship between a type 1 and type 3, who is the achiever, because they are both lacking in emotional attachment to each other and can become competitive with one another. Contention may also arise because Reformers are highly ethical individuals while type 3s do not mind cutting corners if it gets the job done faster and quicker.

Reformers vs. Type 4s

Because of their propensity towards depression, type 1s are often mistaken for type 4s, who are Artists, but type 1s are not nearly as self-indulgent as type 4s. These two are similar in the fact that they are both idealistic and concerned with making things good and right in the world. However, bringing these two together is like mixing water and oil because while type 1 is sensible and objective, Artists tend to see things personally.

Reformers vs. Type 5s

Because they are highly intelligent and independent, Reformers are often mistaken for type 5s, who are deep thinkers who tend to withdraw and observe rather than interact. Reformers are people of action however, not ones to sit back and observe and think. Both of these personality types are usually emotionally withdrawn and find it very difficult to change the basic views on life. Therefore, developing a relationship between these two personality types can be very difficult.

Reformers vs. Type 6s

Type 1s are also mistaken which type 6s, who tend to be anxious, hard-working, and serious-minded people but they differ in the kind of emotional ties that they develop with other people as well as the guidance from their own internal sense of purpose. Type 1s are very reasonable and mentally clear. They are very firm in their decision-making and are able to think clearly under pressure. Therefore, type 1s tend to be leaders. Type 6s, on the other hand, tend to be followers because type 6s become stressed easily and are very doubtful in their decision-making abilities. A relationship between these two personality types may be difficult to develop because type 1s may put too much pressure on type 6s. This can cause resentment and lots of bickering.

Reformers vs. Type 7s

Type 7 is called the Enthusiast and is very different from the Reformer. In fact, the two personality types can be seen as opposites. However, it is these opposites that can make a relationship between them complementary as both bring something that is needed to the table. Type 1s bring orderliness, conscientiousness, attention to detail, and a high standard of excellence while the Enthusiasts brings high energy, curiosity, the desire to try new things, and not get hung up on perfection. Of course, for this same reason, a relationship between these two personality types may be too difficult to develop.

Reformers vs. Type 8s

These two personality types find commonality in the fact that they fight for what is good and just. They both see themselves as Protectors of the weak and fight to make things right. A relationship between the two can be very powerful as it is founded on a clear sense of purpose, and it is decisive and direct. While a relationship between these two is very possible, it is rare that these two form a romantic pair. They find it easier to work as friends or colleagues because they both want to be in charge even though they tend to disagree on the means that should be taken to accomplish a mission. They are both very self-controlled and restrained and find it difficult to express their emotions.

Reformers vs. Type 9s

Both of these personality types would love to bring change to the world. They both tend to put their personal needs aside and work for the welfare of others. They also both believe in delayed gratification. The differences arise in the way that they handle conflicts and confrontation. While type 1s are often openly frustrated with themselves and others and exude a judgmental attitude, type 9s tend to shut down and withdraw, often preferring not to speak about their feelings. In a relationship between these two personality types, this can create a well of resentment and the build-up to a massive explosion of anger.

How the Reformer Can Improve His or Her Life

The Reformer can improve his or her life by practicing self-acceptance. This person needs to realize that along with having many strengths, they also have weaknesses and this is perfectly fine. In addition to accepting that they are not perfect, this person needs to become more self-compassionate. Becoming more mindful allows the Reformer to become more accepting of themselves and more compassionate of their own needs. There are actionable practices that the Reformer can employ to become more in touch with his or her emotions.

Many of these practices involve opening chakras, also called chakra meditation. There are several different types of chakra mediation and each has the power to send energy to particular positions in your body. The effect that they have are enhanced by sounds that are chanted in Sanskrit letters. The chanting causes resonation in the body so that you can feel the chakra movement. The two most common letters to chant are "A," which is pronounced as in "ah," and "M" which is pronounced as "mng" ("ng" like in "king").

Without further adieu, here are a few ways that the Reformer can do these:

- *Practice sacral chakra meditation.* This will allow the Reformer to become more in touch with his or her feelings and develop feelings of passion. The process of doing sacral chakra meditation is simple. Sit in a quiet, relaxing room and place your hands on your lap with your palms up. The left palm goes underneath the right hand. The tip of your thumbs should gently touch. Concentrate on the feeling in your lower back and slowly breathe in and out, chanting on every exhale for up to 10 breaths. This allows you to channel your sacral chakra at the sacral bone at the base of your spine.

- *Practice heart chakra meditation.* This type of meditation helps the Reformer develop compassion towards his or herself and towards others as well. To practice this type of chakra meditation, sit cross-legged on the floor. Allow the tips of your thumb and index fingers to touch on both hands. Place your left hand on your left knee and your right hand just below your breastbone, which is slightly above the solar plexus. Chant as you concentrate on the heart chakra at your spine which is level with your heart.

- *Use acupressure.* Acupressure is an alternative form of therapy that uses the manual application of pressure at certain points on the body that are considered to be lines of energy. This is a practice that has been around for thousands of years and it promotes relaxation and overall wellness. Acupressure practitioners, who are licenced professionals, use their fingers, palms, elbows, and feet to apply this pressure while the recipient lies fully clothed on a soft table. Reformers can find relief with this practice if the practitioner stimulates LIV-3, which is located in the foot on the line between the big toe and the second toe. This stimulation relaxes and unblocks emotions such as repressed anger. The point SP-6, which is located on the inside of the lower leg just above the ankle, can be stimulated to relax, calm, and reduce irritability.

- *Practice mindful yoga.* Mindful yoga is the application of traditional Buddhist mindfulness to connect mind and breath. It allows the practitioner to truly experience the moment. The yoga pose that will be discussed now is called the Hero's pose. To get into it, assume a kneeling posture and sit on your heels. Next place your hands on your thighs, lengthen the tailbone toward the ceiling. Broaden your collar bones so that the shoulder blades move towards each other gently. This will open up your chest. Hold this pose for 1 minute. Allow your mind to clear and focus on the gentle rhythm of your breaths.

Additional practices that the Reformer can use to improve his or life include:

- Taking time out of the day for themselves where there is no need for the accomplishment of anything other than to be in touch with his or her thoughts and feelings.

- Keeping a journal so that he or she can write down their thoughts and feelings, which helps with introspection and reflection.

- Joining group therapy to develop his or her emotions and to realize that others will not condemn them for having needs and weaknesses just like everyone else.

- Practicing patience as they impart their knowledge and wisdom on others.

- Learning to become aware of their irritation at their own shortcomings and the shortcomings of others so that they become less self-critical and undermining of the efforts of others.

- Being careful of the words that they choose when communicating with others so that they do not come across as judgemental.

- Learning to channel their anger in a healthy way because the suppression of anger not only makes for an unhealthy emotional and mental environment but also unhealthy physical health in the form of high blood pressure and ulcers.

- Occasionally indulging in a small treat just for the sake of it.

Chapter 3: The Enneagram Personality Type 2 - The Helper

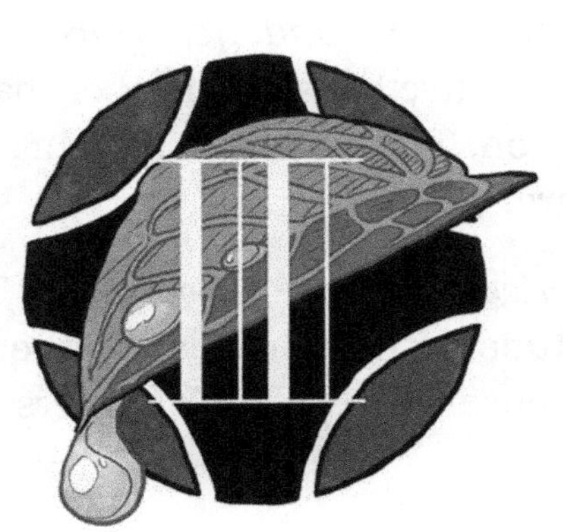

This Enneagram personality type is also called The Giver. This personality type feels that their worth comes from being helpful to others. They are very aware of the needs of others and feel that love is the highest ideal. These people tend to be extroverts and are very socially active because giving to others is their reason for being. If you know someone who always remembers someone else's birthday or goes out of their way to help others then this person is likely a type 2.

What Makes the Helper a Great Personality

1. *The Helper is empathetic.* This personality type is deeply in tune with the needs of others as a result of being able to tune into the energy that other people give off. They often have that instinctive knowhow of when a person is in need of help and is of course, eager to help.

2. *The Helper is thoughtful of the needs of others.* This person is deeply focused in making their relationships with other people work and work tirelessly to support and love the people they develop these relationships with. As a result, most people think of them in a positive way.

3. *The Helper is nurturing and generous.* This person does not hesitate to give the shirt off their backs or lend a shoulder to cry on. This person is a caring personality who loves to share.

4. *The Helper practices genuine self-sacrifice.* This person is so deeply in tune with the needs of others that they often give preference to the needs of others rather than their own needs.

The Deadly Sins of the Helper

1. *The Helper can be intrusive.* Type 2s are deeply emotional and are people who spend a great deal of time developing their personal relationships. Due to the amount of time and energy that they spend, they often expect to be appreciated for their efforts and much of their self-image revolves around how helpful they are to other people. These people need to be needed by others and their love is not entirely without ulterior motive. They often develop a sense of entitlement due to the energy that they expend helping others and feel that they have earned the right to be intrusive if others do not readily cooperate in the way they view things.

2. *The Helper can be possessive.* These people are possessive of the relationships that they have and feel betrayed if the people they have relationships with turn to other people for help instead of them.

3. *The Helper can be manipulative.* As a result of feeling that they are always right in their need to help others and that their way of helping is the best way, this personality type can become quite conniving in the way that they approach dealing with other people. They feel entirely justified in their actions because they feel that they have earned the right because their intentions of being helpful are good. If type 2s do not get their way, they can become hysterical, irrational, and sometimes abusive.

4. *The Helper can be self-neglective.* Due to the fact that they spend most of their time helping other people, they often forget to tend to their own emotional, physical, spiritual, and mental needs. That attention is most often focused on other people and causes them to lose sight of themselves and their own needs. This often leads to burnout. Therefore type 2s need to learn to service themselves as well as others so that they can remain balanced and healthy in all ways.

5. *The Helper can have low self-esteem.* As a result of the focus on other people, Helpers can feel a deflated self of self-worth depending on the approval of others.

How Helpers Relate to Other Personality Types

Helpers vs. Type 1s

Please see Chapter 2: How Reformers Relate to Other Personality Types: Reformers vs. Type 1s.

Helpers vs. Type 3s

Both of these personality types are driven by their emotions even though it is not as obvious with type 3s. They both love attention and have a desire to be loved. As a result, both are people-oriented and love being in the spotlight. This can make a great relationship if the two personality types nurture each other's needs. Unfortunately, a pairing such as this can lead to jealousy and possessiveness because neither type wants to take second place or to let the other shine brighter than them.

Helpers vs. Type 4s

These two can make a warm and affectionate romantic couple since they are both seeking warmth and a genuine connection with someone else. Unfortunately, these two personality types hardly ever form romantic relationships because they can both be too emotional and place too many demands on each other. They more often make great friends and colleagues.

Helpers vs. Type 5s

Type 2s and 5s are complete opposites in the way that they think, what they believe is important in life, and how they approach relationships. When they do form lasting relationships, they are the epiphany of opposites attract. Because type 5s are emotionally distant creatures, Helpers often seen them as a challenge. When a healthy relationship blooms, Helpers bring warmth and ease to the relationship while type 5s bring stability and objectivity. Conflict may arise with the boundaries that these two personality types set for each other and how respectful they are toward each other. Because type 5s are so unresponsive to emotional stimuli, type 2s can become frustrated and hurt by this lack of response. This can trigger anxiety and the type 2's intrusive, manipulative nature.

Helpers vs. Type 6s

Both these personality types take responsibilities in a relationship very seriously. They differ in their approaches. Helpers focus on building intimacy and positivity between the two while the Loyalist focuses on building stability and trust. Because these two personality types are both so responsible, they easily share duties in a relationship. Type 6s value the warmth and generosity that type 2s bring to the table while type 2s value the steadfastness, modesty, and hard-working nature of type 6s. The main problem that these two personality types face in their relationships are issues of control and authority. Types 6s can feel pressure by type 2s to be more decisive. Their help and advice can be perceived as intrusive.

This undermines the type 6s self-confidence, and anxiety and resentment can arise in the relationship.

Helpers vs. Type 7s

These two personality types are similar in many ways such as being extroverted, high energy, their need to make others happy, and being positive. As a pair, these two can excel in their generosity and thoughtfulness toward other people. The issue may arise in the fact that type 2s always want to get closer while type 7s tend to want to wait to settle down. Type 7s do not like limiting their options and while they are capable of maintaining long-term relationships, they tend to hold off for as long as possible. Type 2s can even push them away with their need to hover and become intrusive.

Helpers vs. Type 8s

Both of these personality types are action-oriented, deeply feeling, and Protectors. They bring passion and vitality to the relationship. They help balance each other out. Type 2s are affectionate and appreciate the strength and practicality of type 8s while type 8s love their nurturing and caring qualities. These two work as a pair because their roles in a relationship are so clearly delineated. They are different in their value systems. Type 8s are practical, independent people while type 2s are more sentimental and become more attached. These two personality types normally find conflict in their different philosophies in life.

Helpers vs. Type 9s

Again, these two personality types are similar. They are both nurturing and love healing other people. They are both warm, kind, undemanding, and hospitable. As a pair, they project high energy and provide comfort together. Type 2s are constantly adding new people to the mix to help and this can give rise to stress and conflict. Type 9s prefer matter remain uncomplicated. When these two personality types find balance and make a relationship work, they are a very mellow and generous couple. Problems may arise because both of them prefer to take the backseat in controlling a relation but ultimately someone has to wear the pants. Taking control goes against the nature of both of these personality types. Also both types find it hard to express their feelings and easily grow discontent.

How The Help Can Improve His Or Her Life

Helpers can improve their lives by taking the time for introspection. This self-examination will allow them to get in touch with their own needs so that they can direct some of the energy that they use to tend to others inward.

The Helper can also benefit by letting someone else help them out for a change. This would bring balance to their relationships and help them see that give and take can exist in a healthy accord with each other. Actionable steps that the Helper can use to improve their life include:

- *Practicing root chakra meditation.* This type of meditation helps improve mental stability so that the Helper can deal with their own needs. To do this, the meditation practitioner must let the tips of their thumb and index finger touch then concentrate on the root chakra at the point between the genitals and the anus while chanting.

- *Practicing crown chakra meditation.* This helps develop self-awareness and wisdom. To do this, the practitioner must put their hands on their stomach and let the ring fingers point up so that they touch at the tops. The next step is to cross the rest of the fingers, allowing the left thumb to sit underneath the right. Concentrate on the crown chakra at the top of your head while chanting.

- *Practicing acupressure.* To reduce the effects of having too much emotion on the body, an acupressure practitioner can stimulate the point called P-7, which is located in the middle of the palm side of the wrist in the depression between the two tendons. Stimulating this acupressure point also helps diminish nervousness. The Helper can also be aided by the stimulation of the point ST-36 so that he or she can be more stable in dealing with his or her own needs. This point is located on the front of the leg just below the kneecap in the depression between the shin bone and the leg muscles.

Additionally, the Helper needs to:

- Understand that without first addressing their own needs, they cannot efficiently address the needs of other people.

- Become more conscious of their own motives when they decide to help others so that they help for the sake of helping rather than with an ulterior motive that will set them up for disappointment.

- Ask how a person may need help rather than assuming.

- Communicate their intentions to help before taking action and be willing to accept that a person does not need their help.

- Stop calling attention to the fact that he or she is being helpful and let kindness be its own reward.

- Learn to recognize the affection and love that others give even if they are not in the form that he or she would have perceived as best.

- Volunteer in community activities and homeless shelters where their giving nature will be much appreciated.

- Learn to accept the help of other people.

Chapter 4: The Enneagram Personality Type 3 - The Performer

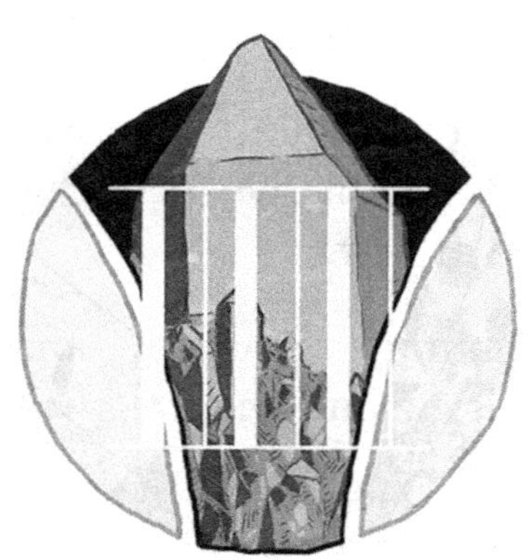

This personality type is also called the Achiever or the Chameleon. This person is driven for success and is determined to achieve their goals no matter what. This person needs to achieve success and to be admired by others so that they feel validated in their worth as individuals. As a result, these people are hard-working, competitive, and highly focused in the pursuit of achieving their goals. These types of people know how to get the job done in the most efficient way possible and always like to celebrate ticking the task off their to-do list.

What Makes the Performer a Great Personality

1. *The Performer is success-oriented.* This personality type is driven to be the best they can be and even likes to motivate others in the same positive way. As a result of this, they are held in high regard by others. The Performer is often the person who is voted the class

president or the one that others should aspire to be like. Because of their drive for success, they are often seen as the embodiment of role models so that others can invest in their own self-development.

2. *The Performer is hard-working.* Because of the need to achieve success, this personality type places a lot of energy in getting the job done.

3. *The Performer is extroverted and outgoing.* Performers are often highly socially competent and extroverted. They are highly charismatic and know how to present themselves to others as self-confident, practical, and driven. They draw energy from crowds and often have that energy that other people find contagious. This results in them being good networkers and often rise very quickly through the ranks because they know how to rub elbows with the best of them.

The Deadly Sins of the Performer

1. *The Performer is image-conscious.* The Performer loves being the center of attention and loves gaining praise from others. Therefore, they often cultivate the way that they look and act to meet the standard that other persons have placed for them. This person wants to be admired and feels a deep sense of loss when they do not feel that this is the case.

2. *The Performer needs external validation.* While the Performer is success-oriented, oftentimes their definition of success is defined by someone else such as their family, social sphere, or culture. They hold the

values and ideas of others in high regard and feel like if they do not meet that standard that they are nobody. They also crave the positive attention and praise that meeting the standard of achievement gains. As a result of this, the Performer can become alienated because they do not know what they truly want or are not truly in touch with their own feelings and interests.

3. *The Performer finds it difficult to form deep emotional ties.* Performers are often secretly afraid of being labeled losers. As a result, they find intimacy with others difficult and because of the need for validation, they often hide a deep sense of shame for who they truly are. These persons often miss out on developing deeply loving relationships and cultivating personal experiences because they are so laser-focused on the outer world and not on nurturing their inner being and the relationships that they form. The fear manifests itself by them pushing others away so that no one gets close enough to unmask the negative feelings that they harbor. This makes types 3s very difficult people to get to know.

4. *The Performer is self-deceptive.* Because of the need for external validation, type 3s are often good at self-deception because even when they appear to be happy, they carry a deep sense of meaninglessness. No matter how strong their social strengths, Performers are often secretly afraid of being labeled losers and overcompensate so that no one else finds out about their deep-rooted fears. Because they are such hard workers, Performers often suffer from burn outs because they do not know when to quit.

5. *The Performer can be unethical.* It is quite common for them to cut corners so that they accomplish their goals in as little time as possible. Even though they are often generous and very likeable people, they can become very ruthless and cold-hearted in the pursuit of excellence and their goals.

How the Performer Relates to Other Personality Types

The Performers vs. Type 1s

Please see Chapter 2: How Reformers Relate to Other Personality Types: Reformers vs. Type 3s.

The Performers vs. Type 2s

Please see Chapter 3: How Helpers Relate to Other Personality Types: Helpers vs. Type 3s.

The Performers vs. Type 4s

These two personality types form a complementary relationship because they play on each other's strengths and compensate for each other's weaknesses. Type 4s can help the Performer access their emotions on a deeper level and help them process their feelings while the Performer can help types 4s handle their emotional reactions with more tact and diplomacy, as well as help ease their self-doubts. Because both of these personality types are both image conscientious they often exude a sense of style and enjoyment for the finer things in life as a couple. Trouble may arise because both of these personality types have self-esteem issues and need attention and validation from external sources. They both harbor questions about their own identity and feel worthless quite easily. This can create a codependency that is unhealthy.

The Performers vs. Type 5s

These two personality types are a frequent combination since type 5s help the Performer gain increased emotional depth, gain expertise in new areas, and become more creative. The Performer helps type 5s get increased self-confidence, better communication skills with others, and better presentation skills. Both of these personality types are focused on their work, are competent and effective. Therefore, they are great at supporting each other while not crowding each other and respecting each other's need for space. As a couple they are well-respected, sharp, and successful. On the flip side of the coin, because of their high competency and focus on work, this can lead to conflict, tension, and elements of competitiveness. Because both of these personality types do not readily speak of their feelings, they can easily grow cold and distant from each other.

The Performers vs. Type 6s

The pairing of these two personality types does not occur often, even though they work very well as a team. Performers bring a hard-working ethic, a desire for communication, ease of connection with other people, and energy to the relationship.

Type 6s introduce support and practical sense to the union. As long as they remain grounded, these two personality types can form a successful and enduring union. Unfortunately these two personality types can also bring out the worst in each other because they have similar negative qualities. They are both very competitive, easily fall into workaholism, look for external sources of validation, and want to be socially accepted. This can give rise to dishonesty, evasiveness, and covert measures to meet their personal needs, which can quickly deteriorate their relationship.

The Performers vs. Type 7s

The pairing of these two personality types are complementary as they are both selfless, high energy, capable in social situations, and outgoing. They bring optimism and future-orientation to the relationship. Even though Performers work alone more readily than type 7s, they are both excellent communicators, persuasive, articulate, and stimulated by the interactions with other people. As a pair, they are generous and fun to be around. Unfortunately, the pair can also be extremely volatile because they are both such high energy types. They also feel a need to project perfection as a couple, which can put a strain on their connection and interaction with each other.

The Performers vs. Type 8s

The pairing of these two personality types can form quite the power couple because they are both assertive and go after the things that they want in life. They often form a pair because they cannot help but notice each other because both shine so brightly as a personality. Even though they are both decisive and strong characters, they tend not to be competitive with each other even though they both have a competitive nature with other people. Their weakness lies in the fact that they both tend to be workaholics and put themselves under a lot of stress in order to achieve their goals. Because they are so focused on achieving their goals, they might not support each other as needed. Type 8s also tend to be controlling, suspicious, and distrusting of others. They may need the Performer to do things that proves his or her loyalty and this results in type 3s feeling used and belittled. This leads to the deterioration of the relationship.

The Performers vs. Type 9s

The pairing of these two personality types is fairly common. Type 9s provide support, encouragement, and pride in the Performer's achievements. Performers help type 9s find value in themselves, develop higher levels of self-respect, and seek investment in their own self-development. The pairing of these two personality types work so well because they are so supporting and accepting of each other. The potential conflict that can arise in this type of relationship is the fact that neither wants to bring up any potential conflicts that they have. This means that problems may fester and introduce fragility into the relationship.

How the Performer Can Improve His or Her Life

The Performer needs to learn to slow down and to form genuine connections with other people as well as get to the heart of his or her true desires. While the Performer does not need to ditch being goal-oriented, this person does need to learn to prioritize goals that benefit them holistically rather than just to gain approval from others. Chakra meditations that are useful to this personality type are the sacral chakra meditation, which is useful in allowing this person to become more in-tune with their feelings, and a heart chakra meditation, which allows for developing compassion and sensitivity internally and externally.

Acupressure application also works for this person. The points that need to be stimulated include:

- *SI-19.* Stimulating this acupressure point allows a person to be more in tune with their heart's desires as well as the hearts of other people. The point is located near the ear just before the small projection in front of the opening of the ear canal.

- *SP-6.* As mentioned before, stimulating this acupressure point, which is found on the inside of the lower leg above the ankle, aids in relaxation and a reduction in irritability.

- *TB-17.* Stimulating this acupressure point helps a person become less sensitive to what other people think about them. It is located behind the ear lobe at the bottom of the ear.

Other ways in which the Performer can improve his or her life include:

- Being honest with his or herself and others about their feelings and needs to project authenticity.

- Resisting the temptation to impress others.

- Resisting performing actions just to be accepted by others. This allows for the discovery of their own core values.

- Learning to develop deeper connections in their relationships. This can be as simple as taking time to have one-on-one conversation with an individual.

- Scheduling breaks in the pursuit of their goals so that they can recharge their battery and improve their outlook on life.

- Pursuing activities that allow for personal advancement rather than just bringing social awareness to themselves.

- Pursuing different types of hobbies so that they can find out what truly resonates with them.

- Resisting the urge to cut corners and remain ethical while pursuing their goals.

Chapter 5: The Enneagram Personality Type 4 - The Artist

Also called the Individualist or the Romantic, the Artist is driven by the need to be unique. This person needs to feel different and special and is constantly on an identity search. This person is trying to build their identity so that they appear different to others and as a result they are often self-conscious. They often see their differences from others as being a gift or a curse because it so sharply sets them apart from others. They see this difference as a gift when it allows them to not fall into a category of commonality with others. They see it as a curse when they feel like it sets them apart from happiness, serenity, and joy.

What Makes the Artist a Great Personality

1. *The Artist is highly expressive.* Because these types of people seek the uniqueness in themselves and in life, they are often highly expressive and turn to creative careers like painting, writing, and other forms of art.

2. *The Artist is self-aware.* The basic desire of the Artist is to find themselves and their significance in this world. They want to create a unique identity for themselves and therefore, strive to do just that. As a result, these personality types often surround themselves with beauty to create moods and feelings that express individuality and express their unique nature. Type 4s also acknowledge and accept their own feelings and do not try to whitewash them. They are not afraid to see their own perceived flaws either.

3. *The Artist is individualistic.* Because of the brutally honest introspection, Artists tend to be true to themselves and develop a high sense of individuality. Type 4s are sensitive souls and often concerned with self-expression and self-revelation. They often outwardly express this with idiosyncrasies in the way that they dress and their overall demeanor.

The Deadly Sins of the Artist

1. *The Artist is misunderstood.* This person is searching for depth in themselves and their relationships and cannot stand shallow interactions and experiences. Because of the differences that they have, Artists often feel superior to others even though they have a feeling of longing and envy because deeply they want to be understood and appreciated by others. This contradiction means that they are misunderstood and underappreciated by others. This also encourages fears of being flawed or defective since they do not fit into the typical mold. This means that Artists are typically

moody and withdrawn from others. Others often perceive them as being temperamental. This can be because they are often in their own internal world where they constantly analyze their feelings. Type 4s often have trouble staying in the moment and can lose themselves in nostalgia.

2. *The Artist often suffers from mental illness.* Because of their overall melancholy disposition, type 4s tend to lapse into depression very easily and can become mentally and emotionally unbalanced because of this self-absorption.

3. *The Artist is often self-indulgent.* They give in to self-indulgence very easily and justify this as a way of compensating for the lack of pleasure in their lives generally. Type 4s are prone to thinking of fantasies to alleviate the problems rather than looking for practical solutions to solve the unhappy.

4. *The Artist is often emotionally disconnected.* Because of the tendency to be stuck in their own head, type 4s often miss out on the joy of participating in a given situation or a given moment. They often feel a deep sense of disappointment when life does not live up to what happens in their heads. They are often easily swept away by their own emotions and feel more comfortable in the darker emotional spectrum rather than the happy light side of things.

How Artists Relate to Other Personality Types

Artists vs. Type 1s

Please see Chapter 2: How Reformers Relate to Other Personality Types: Reformers vs. Type 4s.

Artists vs. Type 2s

Please see Chapter 3: How Helpers Relate to Other Personality Types: Helpers vs. Type 4s.

Artists vs. Type 3s

Please see Chapter 4: How Performers Relate to Other Personality Types: Performers vs. Type 4s.

Artists vs. Type 5s

Both of these personality types are extremely private and, while they may have different interests, they can both appreciate and respect each other's intensity and commitment to their values and feelings. Generally, these two personality types find each other stimulating and are respectful of each other's idiosyncrasies. They inspire each other to be more creative. Conflict may arise because the Artist is more emotional and tends to need deeper contact and intimacy than type 5s. Type 5s tend to push away from emotional attachment because they are thinking types and prefer space in their relationships.

Artists vs. Type 6s

These two personality types are naturally attracted to each other because they are both highly emotional and feel insecure around other people. They are both highly intuitive and as such they are often mistaken for each other. When they both work on the emotional issues, a union between these two personality types is a recipe for steadfast endurance and practicality. Issues may arise between them for the same reason that they are attracted to each other - the deeply emotional nature. Both are very emotionally volatile and can easily feel overwhelmed. They tend to test each other's loyalty and quickly feel a sense of abandonment. Both personality types tend to create self-fulfilling prophecies in their fears and reactions to their relationships.

Artists vs. Type 7s

When these two personality types form a relationship, it is a matter of opposites attracting. Type 4s are emotional, self-doubting, introverted, and quiet while type 7s are more outgoing, confident, extroverted, and optimistic. Type 7s can help the Artist overcome issues of shyness, a reluctance to try new experiences, and to get out of their feelings while the Artist can help the Enthusiast stay focused on the things that they truly want. These two personality types think and react differently but these differences can help them find pleasure in each other. Again, issues may arise because of their differences because they both tend to be impulsive and get easily frustrated with others when they feel that they have been disappointed.

Artists vs. Type 8s

While the Artist is emotionally dominant and type 8 is socially dominant, these two can bring fire and passion into a relationship because they are both highly intuitive, self-aware, and knowledgeable about how they feel. They are both intense personality types and can match each other. Because both types are so reactive, their relationship can be volatile in a negative way with periods of rage, vengeance, and depression. They are prone to having arguments and fights rather than approaching conflict with level heads.

Artists vs. Type 9s

Both of these personality types are withdrawn, private, and emotionally sensitive. They both seek a deep connection with another person and as such can be a supportive pair to each other. Both of these personality types are naturally sensual and love the comfort of being able to express themselves so intimately with someone else. Problems may arise when these two personality types react differently to stressful stimuli. Type 4s can become emotionally volatile while type 9s become withdrawn. These different approaches can make it very difficult to solve conflict in a relationship leading to its deterioration.

How the Artist Can Improve His or Her Life

This person needs to become more grounded in the present moment and to become more in touch with their bodies and less with their emotions. They need to develop a holistic identity and learn to control their emotions rather than being swept away by them. Practicing root and heart chakra meditation helps keep them grounded in reality and become more compassionate towards themselves and others. In addition, they may also practice navel chakra meditation to increase their self-esteem and assertive qualities. Navel chakra meditation starts by putting your hands before your stomach, just below your solar plexus. All fingers need to be joined at the tips. Cross the thumbs and keep your fingers straight. While chanting, concentrate on the navel chakra located on the spine just above the level of the navel.

Acupressure is also helpful. In addition to stimulating the points SP-6 and LIV-3, LI-4 can be stimulated to let go of grief while the stimulation of LU-1 allows for connecting with one's inner worth. L1-4 is found on the top side of the hand between the thumb and index finger where they are connected by the web of Flesh. LU-1 is located on the chest just underneath the shoulder.

Other practical solutions that the Artist can practice to improve his or her life include:

- Not placing so much emphasis on how they are feeling.

- Realizing that their emotions in that moment are limited only to that moment and may not be more important than that.

- Avoiding lengthy conversations with their imaginations, especially if those conversations are excessively negative or resentful.

- Not placing things on the back burner until they are in the right mood.

- Committing to being productive and working consistently in the "real world."

- Pursuing activities that develop their self-esteem and self-confidence.

- Committing to regular sleeping hours and exercise to improve their positivity and outlook on life.

- Practicing self-discipline and avoiding activities that have a negative impact on their lives such as excessive sexual experiences, drugs, alcohol, and sleep.

Chapter 6: The Enneagram Personality Type 5 - The Observer

This personality type is also called the Investigator. This person has a need to understand or to know and is supremely focused on gaining information and knowledge. This person loves to sit on the sidelines and observe from a distance before becoming engaged in new situations, new activities, and new people. They do this because they fear being viewed as incompetent, being unprepared, or being emotionally depleted by disengagement.

What Makes The Observer a Great Personality

1. *The Observer is alert and insightful.* This personality type wants to know why things work the way they do. This person yearns to possess knowledge and to understand their environment. This insight will allow them to defend themselves from threats from that environment. This personality type is always searching,

asking questions, and delving deeper into subjects like the cosmos, the animal kingdom, and the microscopic world. This person does not just accept the opinion of other people but instead conducts their own investigations. They are so mentally grounded, Observers tend to be very intelligent thoughtful on a well-read. As a result, they are often expressed in the areas that capture their interest with many of them being scientifically oriented.

2. *The Observer is often an expert in his or her chosen field.* Observers are often relentless in their pursuit of knowledge and this allows them to easily master many subject areas and interests.

3. *The Observer is independent and innovative.* This personality type does not depend on external validation and thus is very independent in their thinking and the way they live their life. These people are also visionaries because of the broad understanding they have of the world and the way it works.

4. *The Observer is unmanipulative.* Types 5s often come into relationships without agendas and are often simply fascinated by a person, hence their interest in forming a relationship.

The Deadly Sins of the Observer

1. *The Observer fears being useless and incapable.* This person is the epiphany of thinking before acting. Behind their competency is a well of insecurity that stems from being viewed as helpless by other people.

2. *The Observer isolates his or herself.* This person feels most comfortable in the realm of thought because they do not feel secure in their ability to handle life. Therefore, they tend to withdraw to the safety of the mind where they can mentally prepare to deal with other people, situations, and experiences. Type 5s are also reluctant to ask for help from others even though these people will be very happy to help them. These types of people stick to being as self-sufficient as possible.

3. *The Observer gets preoccupied with his or her thoughts and imagination.* While they are extremely smart, Observers have trouble taking the information that they acquire and put it into action even though they are usually very organized in the accumulation of that information. Observers tend to neglect the needs of their bodies, hearts, and spirits because they focus so much of their energy mentally. In their never-ending quest for seeking more information, they sometimes do not apply that knowledge into action and therefore, miss out on a lot of life experiences.

4. *The Observer is emotionally distant.* Observers tend to be comfortable in the realm of thought and so, they are much less connected when dealing with emotions. Therefore, they often have a difficult time handling the demands of relationships and tend to shy away from forming deep connections. They do so because of their sensitivity and feel like they cannot handle the demands of that relationship. This can lead to loneliness. To compensate for this, they often adopt an attitude of intellectual arrogance or careless indifference. While this helps them cope, it often creates an emotional distance between themselves and others and this

distance is often not easily bridged. When they do manage to form deep and meaningful connections with others, type 5s tend to keep lifelong relationships. Even though type 5s have a hard time emotionally expressing themselves, they feel deeply. Because of the deep need for privacy and a fear of intrusion, not many people are aware of the fact that they have so much going on beneath the surface. As a result of this, type 5s tend to have a very minimalistic lifestyle so that their exchange with others and the outside world are kept to a minimum.

5. *The Observer is insecure.* The Observer's need to seek knowledge is often driven by the fact that they feel as if they are ill-equipped to function successfully in the world. They feel inferior in their abilities to do things as well as other people do. Rather than facing this fear, they retreat into their minds. They trick themselves into believing that they can figure things out mentally then rejoin the world better equipped.

How Observers Relate to Other Personality Types

Observers vs. Type 1s

Please see Chapter 2: How Reformers Relate to Other Personality Types: Reformers vs. Type 5s.

Observers vs. Type 2s

Please see Chapter 3: How Helpers Relate to Other Personality Types: Helpers vs. Type 5s.

Observers vs. Type 3s

Please see Chapter 4: How Performers Relate to Other Personality Types: Performers vs. Type 5s.

Observers vs. Types 4s

Please see Chapter 5: How Artists Relate to Other Personality Types: Artists vs. Type 5s.

Observers vs. Types 6s

Both of these personality types are mental types and value accuracy, objectivity, attention to detail, and ability to analyze situations without being biased. The Observer is the more emotionally calm personality type while type 6s are more sympathetic and look for authority in the Observer. The Loyalist's dedication and loyalty can break through the Observer's tendency to isolate his or herself. Potential problems can arise because although both these personality types are mentally inclined, they think differently. Often times this means that they end up on opposite ends of the fence, which can lead to a breakdown in communication and trust.

Observers vs. Types 7s

Both of these personality types are thinking types and have an appreciation for bringing ideas to the relationship. The Observer brings insight, objectivity, and clarity of observation to the relationship and type 7s can bring the enthusiasm for life and spontaneity that the Observer needs to come out of his or her shell. As a result of the tendency of type 5s to emotionally retreat in times of stress, problems may arise because when the pressure rises, type 7s do the opposite and go into hyperdrive and become more emotional. These different coping mechanisms of handling emotional stimuli can cause a rift in the relationship.

Observers vs. Types 8s

A pairing of these two personality types is complementary because they help boost each other's strengths while compensating for each other's weaknesses. Type 8s need to be more self-aware and thoughtful of the impact of their actions on themselves and others, while type 5s need to be more in tune with their bodies and with their environment. The two personality types help balance each other out in a healthy relationship. Both of these personality types are sensitive to rejection and feel rejected easily, which can cause an immediate problem in the relationship. Also, both personality types can be cynical, which can lead to a breakdown in communication.

Observers vs. Types 9s

A relationship between these two personality types can work very effectively because they respect each other's independent nature and allow for both emotional and personal space. Neither is intrusive or hovering. Such a relationship is characterized by respect for each other's boundaries, individuality, and non-intrusiveness. However, there can be too much space between the two personality types, which can cause them to grow apart.

How the Observer Can Improve His or Her Life

This personality type needs to get out of their head and put in the effort to be more intune with their emotional, spiritual, and physical being. They need to realize that making connections with people, engaging in emotional experiences, and stepping out of their heads can make life more enjoyable.

Yoga is a great way to get in touch with your emotions. A great pose to achieve this is called the Child's pose. To achieve this pose, kneel on the floor, sit on your heels, and allow your big toes to touch. With an exhale, lay your torso between your thighs and allow your tailbone to lengthen while you lift the base of your skull away from the back of your neck. Lay your hands on the floor alongside your torso with your thumbs facing up. Rest in this pose for at least 30 seconds and allow your mind to empty itself out. Breathe in and out deeply and feel each breath flow through your body.

Chakra meditations that this personality type can engage in to become more grounded in the present moment and to become more in touch with their emotions includes root chakra, sacral chakra, navel chakra, and heart chakra. Acupressure is also helpful. In addition to the stimulation of the point SP-6 and ST-36, the points TB-5 and KI-6 can be stimulated by an acupressure practitioner. TB-5 can be stimulated to increase sensitivity to feelings and emotions. It is located in the top side of the arm just below the crease of the wrist. KI-6 decreases the effects of fear on the body and is located on the inside of the foot, just below the ankle bone.

Other ways that the Observer can improve their lives include:

- Learning to notice when your mental functioning takes you away from experiencing a moment.

- Staying connected in the present.

- Using exercise as a way to channel nervous energy.

- Not using escapist techniques such as using drugs and alcohol to relax or unwind.

- Taking more decisive actions so that you can increase your self-confidence and self-esteem.

- Learning to cope with conflict by not emotionally withdrawing but by finding healthy solutions.

- Taking the time to become more social and build connections with others.

- Learning to trust in other people by occasionally taking helpful advice so that you can gain a fresh perspective on situations.

Chapter 7: The Enneagram Personality Type 6 - The Loyalist

This personality type is also called the Buddy or The Devil's Advocate. This personality type is very insecure because he or she is often conflicted between trust and distrust and feels very unsteady because of this internal war. Therefore, this person is often very fearful or anxious. As a result, this personality type longs to feel secure and supported.

What Makes the Loyalist a Great Personality

1. *The Loyalist is a problem solver.* This person worries a lot and thinks that everything that can go wrong, will go wrong. As a result, type 6s rarely have peace of mind and are not prone to bouts of spontaneity. This person is very good at troubleshooting because they are often able to see a problem from different points of view. The Loyalist's mind is one that can be a wonderful asset professionally or personally when it is used

appropriately. Because this type of personality is so well-equipped at anticipating problems and finding solutions, they are often prepared for any contingency. They are great at developing structures, systems, and ideas for the things that can go wrong and are often the glue that holds organizations together. Type 6s make great and effective leaders when they can channel the multi-faceted way that their mind works in the right way.

2. *The Loyalist is loyal.* When type 6s enter a relationship, they do not trust easily until that person has proven his or herself. Once they have been given that proof however, they are steadfast in their loyalty. While this can certainly be a good foundation for a relationship, it can do the Loyalists more harm than good sometimes because they stay in a friendship, job, or romantic relationship even when there are signs that they should move on.

3. *The Loyalist is a community builder.* Because they are responsible, trustworthy, self-sacrificing, and reliable, this personality type can create security and stability in the communities around them. They are also very dedicated to the movements they believe in.

The Deadly Sins of the Loyalist

1. *The Loyalist is anxious.* The root of the problems that type 6 experiences stems from the fact that they have lost touch with their own inner guidance and authority and seek to project that control and authority onto someone else. They do not trust themselves and

fundamentally lack faith in their abilities to make the right decisions. Because of the sense of impending doom that they have, they often test their relationships both professionally and personally and create a self-fulfilling prophecy of failure.

2. *The Loyalist is insecure.* Because this person is often torn between trust and mistrust, they are often seeking someone or something that they can believe in that is usually not their own selves. Because they lack that inner guidance, they shuffle back and forth between influence until an influence gains their trust.

3. *The Loyalist has low self-confidence.* Because the Loyalist has this deep-seated need to believe in someone or something, this may give rise to issues of authority as they are often looking to turn over that authority to an external source. They do this because they do not believe that they have the internal knowhow to handle life's challenges by themselves. Also, because they are thinking types, they have issues connecting with their inner guidance system. Therefore, they doubt their own minds and judgment easily.

How Loyalists Relate to Other Personality Types

Loyalists vs. Type 1s

Please see Chapter 2: How Reformers Relate to Other Personality Types: Reformers vs. Type 6s.

Loyalists vs. Type 2s

Please see Chapter 3: How Helpers Relate to Other Personality Types: Helpers vs. Type 6s.

Loyalists vs. Type 3s

Please see Chapter 4: How Performers Relate to Other Personality Types: Performers vs. Type 6s.

Loyalists vs. Types 4s

Please see Chapter 5: How Artists Relate to Other Personality Types: Artists vs. Type 6s.

Loyalists vs. Types 5s

Please see Chapter 6: How Observers Relate to Other Personality Types: Observers vs. Type 6s.

Loyalists vs. Type 7s

These are both mental types and can enjoy mentally stimulating each other with natering, humor, and verbal sparring. They make an effective team because type 6s are great at implementation while type 7s are great at generating new ideas. These two personality types help reinforce each other's strengths in a healthy relationship. Problems may arise when type 7s, who are frightful and do not like to be tied down do not give the type 6s the commitment they crave.

Loyalists vs. Type 8s

These two personality types have issues with trust so when they are able to develop a relationship with a strong foundation, they remain solid. Since they are both mental types, they also bring analytical thinking, foresight, and problem-solving skills to the table. Problems may develop because both these personality types are also emotional but tend to hide their emotions. This can of course foster issues in any type of relationship.

Loyalists vs. Type 9s

Type 6s are often confused with type 9s; however, the difference lies in that type 9s are able to trust in others more easily. Nonetheless, the relationship between the two types is very common and stable because both crave stability and predictability. They can build a relationship on dependable value and hard, honest work. The conflict can come into play because both of these personality types find it hard to emotionally express themselves and can easily become withdrawn.

How a Loyalist Can Improve His or Her Life

The biggest part of improving your life as a Loyalist is to deeply introspect so that you can find your own inner guidance. You need to learn to be more in tune with your inner voice and to trust in that internal guidance. A Loyalist needs to practice making decisions even if they do not have all the answers and move forward without second-guessing themselves.

In addition to practicing root and navel chakra, The Loyalist can practice third eye chakra meditation to gain more power into your own insight. This can also help you establish your own belief systems so that you can rely more on your own judgment. The practice of this kind of chakra meditation involves putting your hand in front of the body just below the breasts so that the middle fingers are straight and touch at the tips, pointing forward. Bend the other fingers so that they touch at the upper two phalanges. The thumbs need to point toward the chest and touch at the tips. Chant while concentrating on the third eye chakra, which is at the point slightly between the eyebrows.

When it comes to acupressure, in addition to stimulating the points SP-6 and KI-6, the points KI-3 and KI-4 can also be stimulated. KI-3 is located on the inside of the foot halfway between the ankle bone and the Achilles tendon. The stimulation of this point helps heal the body from the effects of fear. KI-4 is located on the inside of the foot closer to the Achilles tendon than the ankle bone. Stimulating this point helps this personality type feel more sure of themselves.

In addition, the Loyalist can improve his or her life by:

- Developing the understanding that everyone experiences anxiety and accepting that it is a normal part of life. The exploration will allow for the development of ways to manage it.

- Exploring healthy ways for stress management such as exercise and better quality sleep instead of relying on unhealthy dependencies like alcohol and drugs.

- Practicing deep breathing exercises to dispel anxiety.

- Becoming more aware of your tendency to become pessimistic and to steer away from dark moods.

- Learning to identify what makes you most anxious to prevent from overreacting.

- Realizing that most situations are not as bad as they seem and managing your thoughts so that they do not desolate you.

- Working on being more trusting by taking more risks and confronting your fears in relationship development.

- Telling people how you truly feel about them.

Chapter 8: The Enneagram Personality Type 7 - The Enthusiast

This personality type is also called the Adventurer or The Epicure. This person's attention is focused on positive future planning and the possibilities that the future has to offer. This personality type fears being in pain or deprived and seeks having their desires met.

What Makes the Enthusiast a Great Personality

1. *The Enthusiast is optimistic.* This personality type approaches life with curiosity and a sense of adventure. This means that they are always anticipating the next new thing and look at the world with a "kid in a candy store" outlook. They go on new adventures with a cheerful determination to make the best of it. They are also very grateful and appreciative people because of their many experiences.

2. *The Enthusiast is versatile.* Because this person is eager to experience new things, they can accumulate many new talents and knowledge that makes them able to adapt to new surroundings easily. Because they are multi-talented, Enthusiasts tend to be highly productive and prolific.

3. *The Enthusiast is a fast learner.* They can absorb information like languages and procedures and new experiences quickly. They also tend to have great mind-body coordination and manual dexterity.

4. *The Enthusiast is spontaneous.* Because this person is always looking for their next adventure, they do not spend their time worrying but find a way to gain these new experiences with anticipatory thinking. Therefore, they are usually ready to go on their next adventure even on short notice.

The Deadly Sins of the Enthusiast

1. *The Enthusiast can be undisciplined and impulsive.* Because this personality type is motivated by avoiding and discharging pain, they will usually do whatever it takes to do just that. They can act in a way that is not well-thought out and inconsistent.

2. *The Enthusiast can be out of touch with his or her inner guidance.* When type 7s feel stressed or anxious, they tend to keep busy and search for stimulation through activity to avoid dealing with the reason that caused the distress. Because they are constantly moving from one adventure to another, they often lose touch

with their inner beings and spin their wheels when it comes to making emotional decisions.

3. *The Enthusiast has a fear of not finding his or her sense of purpose.* Because this personality type copes with being out of touch with their other internal guidance system, they compensate by practicing a "trial and error" approach to life. This means that they try several things to find out what suits them best and if they cannot find what satisfies them, they will make substitutions for what they are really looking for.

4. *The Enthusiast can be self-indulgent.* This person can become restless because they are always on the search for a new adventure. This can make them less focused, hyperactive, and unable to say no to themselves.

How Enthusiasts Relate to Other Personality Types

Enthusiasts vs. Type 1s

Please see Chapter 2: How Reformers Relate to Other Personality Types: Reformers vs. Type 7s.

Enthusiasts vs. Type 2s

Please see Chapter 3: How Helpers Relate to Other Personality Types: Helpers vs. Type 7s.

Enthusiasts vs. Type 3s

Please see Chapter 4: How Performers Relate to Other Personality Types: Performers vs. Type 7s.

Enthusiasts vs. Types 4s

Please see Chapter 5: How Artists Relate to Other Personality Types: Artists vs. Type 7s.

Enthusiasts vs. Types 5s

Please see Chapter 6: How Observers Relate to Other Personality Types: Observers vs. Type 7s.

Enthusiasts vs. Type 6s

Please see Chapter 7: How Loyalists Relate to Other Personality Types: Loyalists vs. Type 7s.

Enthusiasts vs. Type 8s

As a couple, these two types can be productive and high energy because of their independent, assertive, and strong-willed nature. Neither type likes postponing their pleasure and tend to be big spenders. They are both generous and seek success. Problems can arise because both resist control and authority. Therefore, they can turn against each other and become defiant.

Enthusiasts vs. Type 9s

This is a common pairing because they are similar and different in their own ways so they complement each other well. Both personality types are friendly, sociable, and have positive outlooks on life. Their ability to forgive and forget means that they can build a strong foundation in a relationship. Potential problems can arise because neither type is good at dealing with the painful aspects of life or a relationship. They would likely only briefly acknowledge a problem before shying away from it. This leaves the problem unsolved which can deteriorate the relationship.

How an Enthusiast Can Improve His or Her Life

This personality type needs to learn to deal with the things that cause them stress and anxiety without using fun and distraction to hide their restlessness. This results in them having a hard time falling asleep and staying up late. This can be aided by the stimulation of acupressure point P-7, which aids in feeling calmer, which facilitates getting to sleep and staying asleep. The stimulation of acupressure points SI-19 and SP-6 also help the Enthusiast focus on and listen to his or her inner being and reduce irritability while promoting relaxation.

The practice of chakra meditations also help with grounding and developing compassion. Practicing root chakra and heart chakra are especially great for this personality type.

Other ways that the Enthusiast can improve his or her life include:

- Recognizing impulsiveness and practicing better judgment before acting.

- Thinking about the long-term consequences over the adventures that you choose to pursue.

- Listening to people more intently to gain new perspectives and thus make better decisions.

- Appreciating silence and solitude more to acknowledge, accept, and deal with anxiety.

- Avoiding the use of addictive substances like stimulants and narcotics to deal with anxiety.

- Getting more quality sleep.

- Choosing quality over quantity when choosing which experiences to pursue so that you can dedicate your full attention to experiencing the moment.

- Taking the time to contemplate your next adventure to ensure that it is really good for you and aids in personal development.

Chapter 9: The Enneagram Personality Type 8 - The Protector

This personality type is also called The Challenger or the Boss. This is a powerful, dominating personality type. As such, this personality type fears being harmed or controlled by other people. They have a need to control their own life and destiny.

What Makes the Protector a Great Personality

1. *The Protector is self-reliant and resourceful.* This personality type enjoys taking on new challenges as well as giving new opportunities to other people. They use the resources that are available to them and use them.

2. *The Protector is protective.* This type of person is courageous and not opposed to putting themselves in danger to protect their vision and other people. People like this perform heroic acts and are common in the police force and fire department. The Protector

develops skills of strength, perseverance, and endurance to ensure that those under his or her protection remain safe.

3. *The Protector is a leader.* This person takes initiative and makes things happen. They are comfortable carrying the load for other people and are natural born leaders because of their decisive and authoritative qualities.

4. *The Protector is independent.* This personality type hates the idea of being indebted to anyone and do not walk the straight and narrow path for the sake of it. They pave their own path and do not bow to social conventions.

The Deadly Sins of the Protector

1. *The Protector has a temper.* This personality type finds it hard to back down from a fight and can become combative. This can make them appear confrontational and intimidating to other people especially if they resort to threats and violence to get their way.

2. *The Protector can become delusional with power.* Because of their natural leadership skills and knowhow in getting things done, this personality type may feel that they are invincible and therefore relentless with their use of power.

3. *The Protector is emotionally defensive.* Being vulnerable is one of the Protectors biggest fears and that includes emotional vulnerability. Therefore, they

have very high emotional walls that are hard to get over. They also feel that deep emotional feelings toward anyone may give that person power over them and they resist attachments such as love.

How Protectors Relate to Other Personality Types

Protectors vs. Type 1s

Please see Chapter 2: How Reformers Relate to Other Personality Types: Reformers vs. Type 8s.

Protectors vs. Type 2s

Please see Chapter 3: How Helpers Relate to Other Personality Types: Helpers vs. Type 8s.

Protectors vs. Type 3s

Please see Chapter 4: How Performers Relate to Other Personality Types: Performers vs. Type 8s.

Protectors vs. Types 4s

Please see Chapter 5: How Artists Relate to Other Personality Types: Artists vs. Type 8s.

Protectors vs. Types 5s

Please see Chapter 6: How Observers Relate to Other Personality Types: Observers vs. Type 8s.

Protectors vs. Type 6s

Please see Chapter 7: How Loyalists Relate to Other Personality Types: Loyalists vs. Type 8s.

Protectors vs. Type 7s

Please see Chapter 8: How Enthusiasts Relate to Other Personality Types: Enthusiasts vs. Type 8s.

Protectors vs. Type 9s

Type 9s often admire the take charge qualities that the Protector brings to the table while Protectors like being around other people that are impressed by their leadership. Therefore, these two types gravitate toward each other. Protectors luxuriate in the calm that type 9s bring and the two types find safe harbor in each other even though the relationship between them can be described as one of fire and ice. In a relationship, their roles are well-defined and they are both powerfully driven. Problems can arise because these two react differently to emotional stimuli. While type 8s push harder to restore balance, type 9s tend to shut down.

How a Protector Can Improve His or Her Life

Because this personality type gets angered easily, they often suffer the unhealthy consequences that this can create in the body even though it makes them feel strong and empowered. Type 8s can benefit from realising that anger does not empower them but that it leaves them at the mercy of their heated emotions. Practicing acupressure can help alleviate those unhealthy feelings and their consequences. Stimulating both point LIV-2 and point LI-11 aid in this. LIV-2 is located on the top part of the foot between the big toe and second toe while LI-11 is found on the side of the elbow on the outer side of the arm.

Practicing chakra meditation, specifically crown, heart, and third eye chakra, benefits type 8s by allowing them to focus on compassion and kindness instead of fighting. This allows them to practice thinking before acting.

Other ways that the Protector can improve his or her life is by:

- Acting with restrain even when they feel anger.

- Using breathing techniques to control the flow of anger through the body.

- Using tools like stress balls to control the flow of anger.

- Using their power of inspiration and natural leadership to move them to action instead of using brute force.

- Not allowing their ego to become inflated and allow others to help occasionally.

- Allowing others to show them affection and openly do the same as well.

- Allowing themselves to see that not everyone is against them.

- Realising that while many rely on their power and leadership, they also need the support of other people in their quests.

Chapter 10: The Enneagram Personality Type 9 - The Peacemaker

This personality type is also called the Mediator. This personality type has a stable inner peace that helps them create harmony and balance around them. Their biggest fear is that of loss and separation. They therefore avoid conflicts as much as possible and steer clear of things that can upset them.

What Makes the Peacemaker a Great Personality

1. *The Peacemaker is self-aware.* This personality type is dedicated to the pursuit of inner and outer peace with not only themselves but other people too. Therefore, they are very in tune with themselves and not ones to get easily overwhelmed by their emotions. They often feel fulfilled.

2. *The Peacemaker is spiritual.* They are spiritual in nature and long for a connection with the rest of the universe. This makes them very connected with their inner beings. This helps type 9s stay optimistic and easy-going because they tend to go with the flow.

3. *The Peacemaker is supportive and trusting.* Peacemakers tend to see the best in other people and go

with their gut often. Therefore, they are quick to offer support and are quick to trust.

4. *The Peacemaker holds the community together.* Type 9s have a penchant for problem solving because they are usually able to see things from different points of view. That makes them great mediators and communicators, which allows them to bring people together peacefully. They also have a calming and healing influence on other people.

The Deadly Sins of the Peacemaker

1. *The Peacemaker can be too complacent.* Because this personality type likes keeping the peace, they can over simplify problems and try to minimize the effect these problems have on them. This makes them sometimes too willing to go along with other people just to avoid causing conflict.

2. *The Peacemaker does not like change.* This personality type hates the idea of conflict and will do almost anything to avoid it. Therefore, even though they are easy-going, they have a conservative approach to change because of the disruptive feelings it can cause in them. They often handle this by becoming disengaged with the moment. However, when type 9s do have to deal with change, they are very adaptive and resilient.

3. *The Peacemaker does not handle anger well.* This personality type tends to not give themselves enough credit. This also makes others take them for granted, which can create anger that this type tries to suppress.

This anger can erupt in bouts of temper and passive aggressive behavior. This can also make the Peacemaker stubborn and stuck in their ways.

How Peacemaker Relate to Other Personality Types

Peacemakers vs. Type 1s

Please see Chapter 2: How Reformers Relate to Other Personality Types: Reformers vs. Type 9s.

Peacemakers vs. Type 2s

Please see Chapter 3: How Helpers Relate to Other Personality Types: Helpers vs. Type 9s.

Peacemakers vs. Type 3s

Please see Chapter 4: How Performers Relate to Other Personality Types: Performers vs. Type 9s.

Peacemakers vs. Types 4s

Please see Chapter 5: How Artists Relate to Other Personality Types: Artists vs. Type 9s.

Peacemakers vs. Types 5s

Please see Chapter 6: How Observers Relate to Other Personality Types: Observers vs. Type 9s.

Peacemakers vs. Type 6s

Please see Chapter 7: How Loyalists Relate to Other Personality Types: Loyalists vs. Type 9s.

Peacemakers vs. Type 7s

Please see Chapter 8: How Enthusiasts Relate to Other Personality Types: Enthusiasts vs. Type 9s.

Peacemakers vs. Type 8s

Please see Chapter 9: How Protectors Relate to Other Personality Types: Protectors vs. Type 9s.

How a Peacemaker Can Improve His or Her Life

The Peacemaker's need to keep the peace often means that they do not assert themselves and make their voice heard. To help boost this personality type's self-expression abilities, practicing chakra meditation is helpful. Throat chakra meditation is done by crossing the fingers on the inside of the hands and letting the thumbs touch at the tips. Pulling the thumbs apart slightly, concentrate on the throat chakra at the base of the throat and chant. Navel chakra meditation is also useful for developing assertiveness, while sacral helps the Peacemaker become more passionate and crown chakra helps develop self-awareness.

The stimulation of GB-44 helps with decisiveness and focus, while stimulating LIV-1 helps with assertiveness. GB-44 is located on the fourth toe in the outer corner of the nail. LIV-1 is located on the big toes at the bottom corner of the nail.

Other strategies the Peacemaker can use to help improve their lives include:

- Not overeating or undereating to deal with repressed anger. Instead acknowledge it and deal with it.

- Exercising to deal with anxiety and to boost happiness and fulfillment. This allows for being more in tune with emotions and the body.

- Recognize anxiety and causes for anger in their lives and channel it in a positive way.

- Actively paying attention to what is going on in the environment and not allowing daydreaming to disengage from change or discomfort.

- Developing schedules and structure to stay on top of priorities and to remain engaged in the moment.

- Engaging in activities that help develop self-esteem and self-confidence.

- Develop conflict resolution skills to handle conflict in a healthy way instead of avoiding it.

- Taking more risks to become more comfortable with change.

Conclusion

Everyday we go through experiences and have thoughts and feelings that change us but fundamentally we remain who we are because our personality types are unchanging. Our careers, relationships, and health change. The seasons change and we experience tragedies and moments that give us great joy. Knowing and understanding our personality type and therefore, who we are deep inside, helps us persevere and find the best way to handle these changes, whether good or bad.

After all the information that has been given in this book, I bet that you are eager to find out what your personality type is if you have not already figured it out. Look below for 20 questions that will you help you find out the truth.

How to Find Out Your Personality Type

1. Am I a perfectionist or am I more accepting of imperfection?

2. Am I demanding or undemanding?

3. Am I ordinary or different?

4. Am I rule abiding or will I break the rules if they are a means to an end?

5. Am I loyal or not much into commitment?

6. Am I sociable or not?

7. Am I caring or indifferent?

8. Am I generous or stingy?

9. Do I have trouble staying no or do I say no easily?

10. Do I go with my gut feeling often or ignore these feelings?

11. Am I diligent or do I get distracted easily?

12. Am I individualistic or do I work well in teams and groups?

13. Am I cautious or adventurous?

14. Am I disciplined or undisciplined?

15. Am I energetic or low energy?

16. Do I withdraw from people or do I gravitate toward other people?

17. Am I meticulous or uncritical?

18. Am I domineering or treat other people as equals?

19. Do I often help others or leave them to their own devices?

20. Do I need to be successful or not?

By taking the time to answer these questions, you can compare the answers to the personality types in this book and find the ones you most closely relate to.

You can also take the free test available at https://www.enneagraminstitute.com/ for a better understanding of your personality type.

A Final Word

The information given in this book may be overwhelming to some people at first but it is relevant in helping you start that journey of self-development. This journey is not individualistic and will involve you examining your relationships and the environments you function in. As mentioned before, you might become scared, angry, and sad but you will be rewarded with joy and fulfillment. Be courageous and take the first steps in that journey, which is finding out your personality type by making use of this ever useful Enneagram system. I wish you luck in developing yourself and the relationships in your life. You will be all the happier, more fulfilled, and successful because of it.